A Great Idea
ENGINEERING

The
Pyramids of Giza

by Don Nardo

NORWOOD HOUSE PRESS

COVER: The Great Pyramids of Giza, Egypt.

Norwood House Press
P.O. Box 316598
Chicago, Illinois 60631

For information regarding Norwood House Press, please visit our website at:
www.norwoodhousepress.com or call 866-565-2900.

Paperback ISBN: 978-1-60357-573-7

The Library of Congress has cataloged the original hardcover edition with the following call number: 2013010630

Manufactured in the United States of America in North Mankato, Minnesota.
233N—072013

Contents

Chapter 1:
Trouble with Tomb Robbers   4

Chapter 2:
How the Pyramids Were Built   14

Chapter 3:
Objects of Mystery and Wonder   25

Chapter 4:
The Pyramids in Later Ages   35

Glossary   44

For More Information   45

Index   47

About the Author   48

Note: Words that are **bolded** in the text are defined in the glossary.

Trouble with Tomb Robbers

On a flat, sandy stretch of land near Egypt's capital city, Cairo, three massive mounds tower into the sky. The place, called Giza, is famous worldwide. This is because these stone mountains are not natural features. Rather, they were made by human hands. The people who built them had no modern-style tools or machines. In a truly amazing feat, the ancient Egyptians managed to move millions of stone blocks.

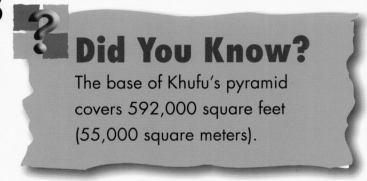

Did You Know?

The base of Khufu's pyramid covers 592,000 square feet (55,000 square meters).

Each weighed several tons. Somehow they stacked them, layer upon layer, higher and higher.

The result is the famous Pyramids of Giza--those of the pharaohs Khufu, Khafre, and Menkaure.

Tourists are dwarfed by Khufu's enormous pyramid.

They are masterpieces of construction. The largest of the three structures, the great pyramid of Khufu, stands an astounding 481 feet (147m) high. That is about the height of a 48-story skyscraper. It is also more than three times taller than New York's Statue of Liberty. In fact, Khufu's pyramid remained the tallest human-made building on earth until modern times. It is no wonder that it was named one of the seven wonders of the ancient world.

The Earliest Royal Tombs

Khufu was one of ancient Egypt's first **pharaohs**, or kings. The pyramid that bears his name was his tomb. After Khufu died in 2566 BC, he was placed inside the

Changing Beliefs About the Afterlife

At first, the Egyptians believed that the pharaohs were living gods. As such, they were the only humans who could reach the afterlife and live forever. Later, well after Khufu's day, religious ideas changed. The Egyptians accepted that all people, both rich and poor, might make it into the afterlife. There they would enjoy eternal peace in the Underworld, a realm ruled by the god Osiris.

The god Osiris ruled the underworld and all Egyptians believed they might make it to the afterlife.

pyramid. Since then, almost 46 centuries have passed. That is nearly 20 times longer than the United States has been a country!

Back in Khufu's time, building huge stone pyramids seemed to be the solution to an important problem. Namely, how could the bodies and **grave goods** of the pharaohs be kept safe? Their grave goods consisted of expensive clothes, furniture, eating utensils, tools, weapons, and much more. The ancient Egyptians believed that a pharaoh would need these items in the afterlife.

The trouble was grave robbers. They looted the royal tombs in which the grave goods were placed. At first, the pharaohs and other wealthy nobles were buried in structures called **mastabas**. The word *mastaba* means "bench" in Arabic. Small

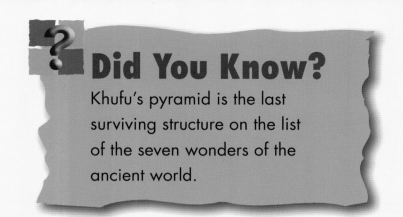

Did You Know?

Khufu's pyramid is the last surviving structure on the list of the seven wonders of the ancient world.

benches stood beside the front doors of many Egyptian homes. And mastabas looked a lot like those benches.

The problem was that mastabas, made of mud and clay, were not strong or permanent enough. First, the effects of rain and wind steadily made the flimsy mud bricks crumble. As a result, the mastabas had to be repaired on a regular basis. Even worse, tomb robbers easily tunneled through the walls. They helped themselves to the precious objects meant for the deceased.

Khufu's Record Finally Broken

When first built, the great pyramid of Khufu was an impressive 481 feet (147m) tall. No one built a structure that rivaled it in size during ancient times. Nor was its height surpassed in the Middle Ages. Not until 1884, less than a century and a half ago, was its record broken. That was the year that the Washington Monument, in Washington, DC, was built. At 555 feet (169m), it is 74 feet (22m) taller than Khufu's tomb

The First Pyramid

A major step toward making royal tombs more permanent and safe occurred

The first Egyptian pyramid, Djoser's step pyramid, pictured here, was designed and built by Pharaoh Djoser's vizier Imhotep around 2667 BC.

almost a century before Khufu was born. In about 2667 BC, a man named Djoser (ZOH-ser) ascended Egypt's throne. He chose as his **vizier** a man named Imhotep. Egyptian viziers had an important job and held much power. They ran the government and put the pharaohs' policies into practice.

Appointing Imhotep vizier turned out to be a wise move. He was a talented architect and builder. Imhotep began planning Djoser's tomb. The vizier wanted it to be sturdy enough to discourage would-be thieves. So he used two new approaches. The first was to make the mastaba much larger than normal. Perhaps he thought that a bigger tomb would take more time and effort to break into. The first mastaba Imhotep built was huge.

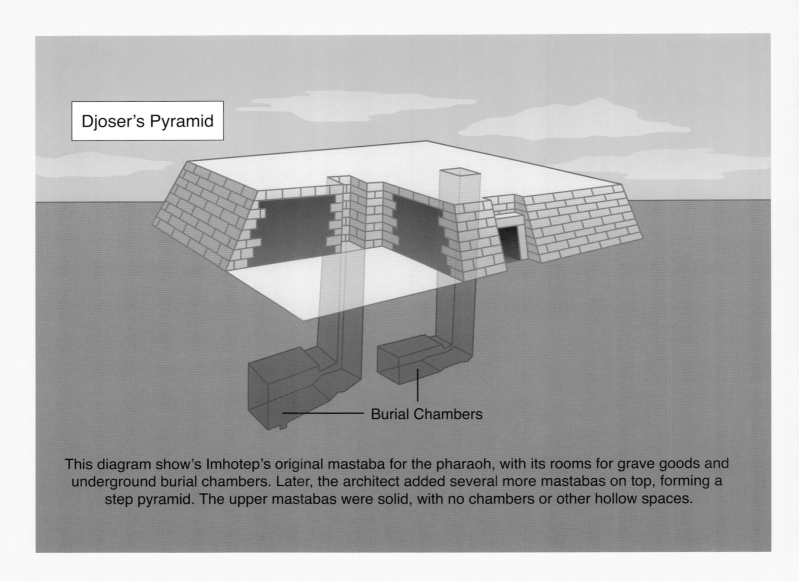

Djoser's Pyramid

Burial Chambers

This diagram show's Imhotep's original mastaba for the pharaoh, with its rooms for grave goods and underground burial chambers. Later, the architect added several more mastabas on top, forming a step pyramid. The upper mastabas were solid, with no chambers or other hollow spaces.

It was 207 feet (63m) on each of its four sides. That made it more than two-thirds of a football field in length. It was also 26 feet (8m) high—a bit taller than a modern two-story house.

Imhotep's second new approach was to use stone rather than brick. He knew that building with stone was more costly and difficult. But the tomb would be a lot stronger and more enduring. Workers started to follow Imhotep's design and built the all-stone mastaba at Saqqâra, near Egypt's capital of Memphis.

At that point, everyone thought that Djoser's tomb was finished. But they were wrong. Imhotep suddenly had what he thought was an even better idea. He said he could make the tomb stronger still. He decided the way to do this was

Dating Egypt's Pyramids

The time period often called the Pyramid Age lasted from the start of Djoser's reign, in 2667 BC, to about 2180 BC. These five centuries happened at the same time as the Old Kingdom. This is the name given to ancient Egypt's first major historical age. It lasted from 2686 BC to 2181 BC. The Old Kingdom was followed by the Middle Kingdom (2055 BC to 1650 BC) and New Kingdom (1550 BC to 1069 BC). Some pyramids were built in the Middle and New Kingdoms and even a bit later. But they were far fewer and smaller than those of the Old Kingdom.

to create a stack of mastabas. Again with Djoser's approval, he built a total of six mastabas, one on top of another. The biggest was at ground level. And each one in the stack was a little smaller than the one below it.

The final structure was the world's first pyramid-tomb. Each of the six levels formed what looked like a giant step. So it became known as the Step Pyramid of Saqqâra. The original building was 413 feet (126m) long and 344 feet (105m) wide at the base. Its height was 200 feet (61m).

The Pyramid Age

In the years that followed, several more step pyramids were built to house the remains of pharaohs. Each of these structures used stone and were made of large mastabas piled atop one another. But some royal architects had ideas for changes. At some point, one of them— whose name is lost to history—decided to get rid of the steps. He filled them in with more stone blocks. Also, he extended the flat roof of the top level to a point. The result was the first smooth-sided, or "true," pyramid.

Khufu's father, Sneferu, had built several true pyramids. But these were a lot smaller than Khufu's and that of his son, Khafre. The largest ever built in Egypt, the two were built beside each other at Giza.

Khufu's tomb, then called Akhet-Khufu, or "Khufu's Horizon," was truly huge. At 756 feet (230m) on each side, its base covered more than 13 acres (5.3ha). It was only 3 feet (91cm) taller than Khafre's

Khufu's son Khafre built the second-largest pyramid in Egypt, pictured here.

pyramid, which stood 478 feet (146m) high. The third Giza pyramid, built for Khafre's successor, Menkaure, was quite a bit smaller than the other two. It was only 220 feet (67m) tall. Yet it was much bigger than the tomb Imhotep had built for Djoser.

In all, Egypt's pharaohs built more than 90 pyramids. Most were completed during the five-century period lasting from about 2667 BC to 2180 BC. For this reason that era is often called the Pyramid Age. How these structures were built has fascinated people ever since.

Chapter 2

How the Pyramids Were Built

Today people from around the world regularly visit the pyramids at Giza. Almost always, they are awed by the huge size of these monuments. Often they pepper their tour guides with questions. How many separate blocks are there in Khufu's pyramid? How did people lacking modern-style tools and machines manage such a feat? How did they lift those huge stone blocks to the upper levels? And were those who did the lifting slaves or free Egyptians?

Slaves or Free Workers?

Archaeologists and historians have tried to answer these questions for a long time. Answering the last question first, they say that the workers were not slaves. That mistaken notion, they explain, comes mostly from movies. Cecil B. DeMille's

Workers dig at a site near the Giza pyramids. The tombs of some of the workers who helped build the pyramids were unearthed at the site.

1956 film *The Ten Commandments* is a famous example. It shows hordes of slaves toiling in misery to build a new city for a cruel pharaoh. Many film-goers have just assumed that slaves also built the pyramids.

That notion also came from the fifth-century-BC Greek historian Herodotus. While he was visiting Egypt, local tour guides told him that the pharaoh Khufu enslaved some of his own people. Then he forced them "to drag blocks of stone from the quarries." The slaves worked "in three monthly shifts, a hundred thousand men in a shift," Herodotus reported.

Though he meant well, Herodotus got it wrong. And so did his guides. They were probably not lying, however. The problem was that the Giza pyramids had arisen more than 2,000 years before the

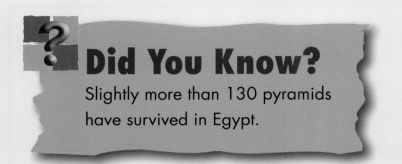

guides were born. After all that time, no one remembered exactly when or how those structures were built. Nor did anyone recall the identity of the workers. By Herodotus's time, everyone simply assumed they had been slaves.

Not until modern times did experts uncover evidence showing that the workers were actually free Egyptians. Most of them were farmers. They grew crops like wheat, beans, and lettuce. They also raised pigs and other domesticated animals. Their farms were located in the well-watered areas near the Nile River's banks. Between the planting and harvest seasons, the farmers had some free time on their hands. It was then that some of them worked on government construction projects.

Where the Workers Lived

Most of these workers lived too far from Giza to commute back and forth each day. So the government put up temporary housing for them near the worksite. A small workers' village was found right on the Giza plateau in the 1990s. Evidence suggests that most of the houses were much like the farmers' own modest homes. They were made from

Egyptian masons dress and lay blocks for a pyramid.

mud bricks, river reeds bound into tight bundles, or both.

Archaeologists also found the remains of bakeries at Giza. These made bread for the workers each day. The chief excavator, Zahi Hawass, describes one bakery. "Along the east wall," he writes, "were two lines of holes in a shallow trench, resembling an egg carton. The holes had held dough-filled pots, while hot coals and ash in the trench baked the bread."

In addition, Hawass and his colleagues found cemeteries near the village. These contained the graves of workers and members of their families. When one of them died while working on the nearby pyramids, they were buried in these cemeteries.

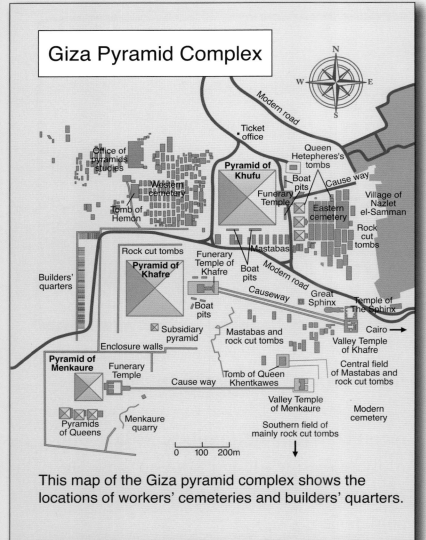

Giza Pyramid Complex

This map of the Giza pyramid complex shows the locations of workers' cemeteries and builders' quarters.

At the Worksite

After awakening and having breakfast each morning, the workers joined their construction gangs. These were groups of men who regularly labored together. They usually did the same job each day. Some gangs, called **zaa**, had 200 men each. Members came up with some descriptive nicknames for their groups. Among them were Boat Gang, Enduring Gang, North Gang, and South Gang.

The tools these workers used on the job were very basic by modern standards. Many were made of stone. These included stone axes, knives, picks, chisels, and saw blades. Some copper knives and saws were also used. The hammers some of the workers used were made of either stone or wood. With such tools, little by little they cut and trimmed the big stone blocks needed to build the pyramids. Some 2.3 million of these blocks were used to build Khufu's tomb.

Other common tools the workers used were wooden **levers** and **sledges**. A sledge was basically a large sled. With these, they moved the heavy stones to and around the worksite. An average stone weighed a whopping 2.5 tons (2.3t). Members of a work gang placed a sledge beside a stone they wanted to move. Using several levers and a lot of muscle power, they tilted the stone up and onto the sledge. Then they attached ropes to the sledge and dragged it across a bed of

Quarrying the Stones

The stones for the Giza pyramids came from various quarries. To remove a stone from a quarry, workers first softened the stone's surface. They did this by creating sudden temperature changes. They dumped hot coals onto the stone and waited till it was very hot. Then they poured cold water over the stone. When the surface was soft enough, they went to work with chisels and hammers. Pounding away, they cut grooves deeper and deeper. Eventually, they freed the stone from the quarry and dragged it away toward the worksite.

wooden rollers. Some workers picked up rollers the sledge had already passed over. Then they ran around and laid them down in front of the sledge.

Workers used ropes and rollers to move large stones up ramps next to the pyramid.

The first stones were used to build a pyramid's foundation. It had to be perfectly level. Otherwise, the finished structure would later shift, crack, or maybe even collapse. They managed to level the foundation of Khufu's tomb with amazing precision. The difference in flatness from one side of the pyramid to the other is a mere three-quarters of an inch (2cm)!

The Workers' Incentives

It appears that the free citizens who worked on the pyramids had several incentives. First, such work seems to have fulfilled some or all of their tax duties. Also, the government fed the workers while they were on the job. The government may also have given food to workers' families while they waited for harvest time. Finally, evidence suggests that people saw it as an honor to help the pharaoh reach the afterlife. What is certain is that this kind of labor was very common in ancient Egypt. In fact, most Egyptians did it at least once in their lifetime.

Raising the Stones

On top of this well-constructed base, the workers began adding layers of stone blocks called **courses**. Installing the first and lowest course was the easiest. They dragged the sledges with the stones to the desired spots. Using levers and muscle power again, they eased the stones into place.

Raising the stones for the higher courses was a great deal harder. Historians still debate how it was done. One theory suggests the workers built huge ramps made of sand and stone debris along the structure's sides. They then dragged the loaded sledges up the ramps.

Another, more recent theory was proposed by English master builder Peter Hodges. He performed experiments with 2-ton (1.8t) stone blocks. As few as two men were able to lever up one end of such a block. They quickly pushed wooden wedges under that raised end. They then did the same thing on the block's

Raising the Stones

Peter Hodges's jack-up procedure for raising 2-ton blocks for a pyramid. This enabled stones to be lifted several inches in a few minutes.

1 The levers are put in position for the first jack.

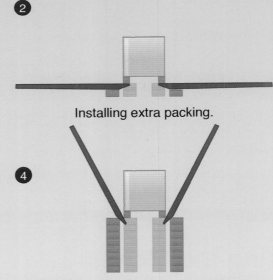

2 Installing extra packing.

3 Extra packing below the levers. Start the next jack.

4 Repeat this sequence until 8 packings are inserted and start the horizontal movement.

opposite side. In only a few minutes, they had raised the block several inches. Repeating this process a few more times, the two men moved the block as high as an average course of Khufu's pyramid. Hodges thinks that dozens of such two-man teams were using this method at any given moment during a workday.

Many experts agree with Hodges. This is because his proposed method sounds a lot like the one Herodotus described. He wrote that the stone blocks "were lifted from the ground level by [levers] made of short timbers." Another team of workers "raised the blocks a stage higher, then yet another which raised them higher still. Each tier, or story, had its set of levers."

In this or a similar manner, only a few thousand workers laid down course

Leveling the Foundation

Most modern experts agree on how the workers made a pyramid's foundation level. First, they painted marks on the ground where they wanted the structure to sit. Then they drove wooden stakes into the ground along the sides of that outline. Next, they tied long cords to the tops of the stakes so that the cords criss-crossed the site. When the upper surfaces of the foundation stones touched the cords, the workers knew that those stones were level. To make sure, the workers used similar **horizontal** cords to test each succeeding course of stones.

after course of stones. As they did so, they placed the outermost stones in each course inward by the width of one stone. In that way, the ascending courses slanted inward, producing the structure's triangular form.

Workers were grouped together in gangs, called *zaa*, which regularly labored together.

The builders were able to accomplish these steps using the most basic of tools. When all the courses were laid, they added the casing stones. These were sheets of smooth, white limestone. The stones fully sheathed the pyramid, giving it a solid, polished outer surface. (Most of these outer stones are now gone. People in later ages removed them to use in making smaller buildings.) The workers who built and gazed on these structures in their original glory are long gone. But most of the fruits of their labor have stayed intact for future generations to admire.

Chapter 3

Objects of Mystery and Wonder

The Giza pyramids' great size and shiny casing stones were only part of what made them amazing creations. To the Egyptians, their very shape had deep religious meaning. So did the direction their doors faced in relation to the sky. The burial chambers and royal remains hidden inside these structures were also objects of religious mystery and wonder.

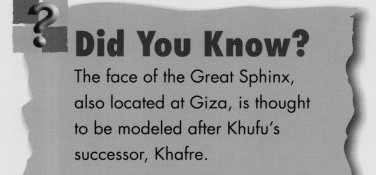

? Did You Know?

The face of the Great Sphinx, also located at Giza, is thought to be modeled after Khufu's successor, Khafre.

The builders included various religious aspects when making the pyramids. This was because the Egyptians were very

A detail from an Egyptian tomb shows some of the gods the Egyptians worshipped. Egyptian religion had a wide range of gods and many public festivals and holidays.

Religious temples ran large-scale estates staffed with hundreds of people. Architecture, painting, sculpture, and music were strongly influenced by religion. And public festivals and holidays honoring the gods were major social events.

spiritual people. As Herodotus wrote, "They are religious to excess, beyond any other nation in the world."

Evidence shows that Egyptian culture was full of religious ideas and customs. Nearly everyone believed in and worshipped a wide range of gods.

Spiritual, Mystical Elements

As the tombs of semidivine rulers, the pyramids also contained religious concepts and **symbols**. These began with the pyramids' shape. The way the royal architect Imhotep had stacked his six mastabas to form the first pyramid had not been an accident. He knew that the pyramid shape had several religious or mystical meanings to Egyptians. For instance, they believed that a pyramid was shaped like the original mound of creation. Called the **ben-ben**, in Egyptian mythology it was first land to appear on earth. The belief was that a mighty creator-god named Atum had fashioned it.

Another belief about pyramids was that they stood for invisible stairways to the heavens. People believed the pharaoh's soul, or spirit, went up such a stairway. Eventually, they believed, his spirit would become one with the sun's rays. Then he would enter the gods' heavenly kingdom.

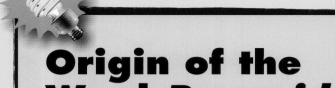

Origin of the Word *Pyramid*

Although the Egyptians built the first pyramids in the world, the word *pyramid* is not Egyptian. In the Egyptian language, the word for something pyramid-shaped is *mer*. The term *pyramid* is Greek. It came from the ancient Greek word *pyramis*, which means "wheat cake." Greeks first laid eyes on the Giza pyramids more than 1,000 years after they were built. Maybe they felt they looked like giant wheat cakes sitting in the desert.

Egypt's oldest known **funerary** writings, the Pyramid Texts, described this process. "A ramp to the sky is built for him," they said about the pharaoh. That way, "he may go up to the sky." There,

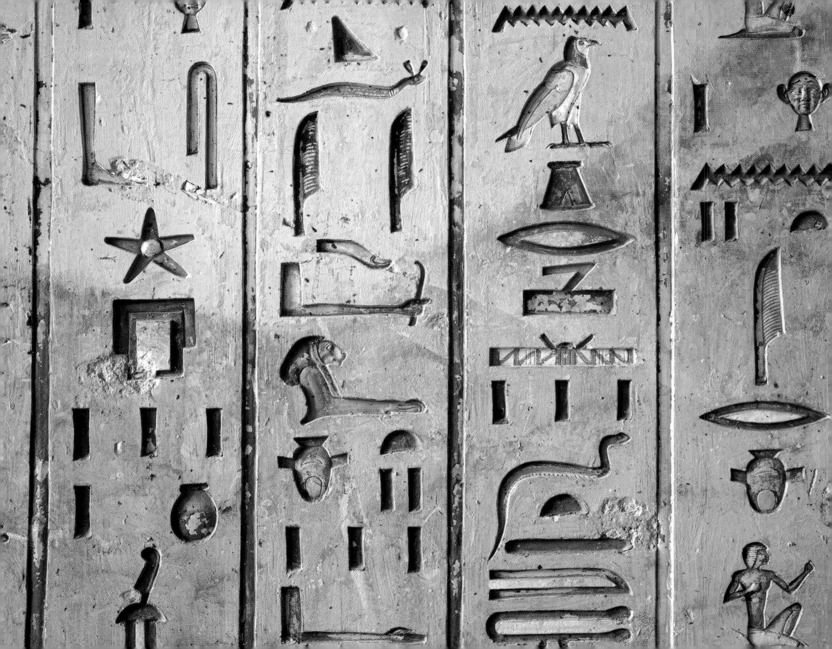

"he has taken his stand with Ra," the sun god, "in the northern part of the sky."

Another way the Giza pyramids were religious was how they were set up. The builders placed them on the plateau in a specific way. The four sides of each pyramid point directly at the four **cardinal points**. These are north, south, east, and west.

The builders also made sure to put the main door of a pyramid in the center of its north-facing side. Some modern experts think this was done to help the pharaoh's soul reach heaven. The Egyptians believed that most gods dwelled in the northern part of the sky. So **aligning** a pyramid so its door faced due north gave the dead king's spirit the clearest path to that goal.

Sacred Interior Spaces

Religious mystery also surrounded the passages and chambers inside the pyramids. First, people viewed these interior spaces as very sacred areas. This was partly because they were part of tombs for special, semidivine people. Also, a pyramid's burial chamber was like a launching pad. It marked the starting point of the journey of a king's soul to heaven. One historian called Khufu's pyramid "a machine for **resurrection**."

Khufu's tomb at Giza is a good example of how a pyramid's interior spaces

Hieroglyphics adorned the interior of the tombs. These hieroglyphics are from a tomb drawing found in the Pyramid Texts.

Creating the Sacred Mound

The Egyptians believed that the ben-ben first arose at Heliopolis. This was a town that was a few miles northeast of Giza. The priests of Heliopolis's main temple told a story of how the mound appeared. The universe was at first a monstrous mass of dark, swirling waters, they claimed. But at some point a miracle occurred. In a way no one could explain, the great god Atum sprang into existence. He then created the first land—the ben-ben. That sacred mound was shaped much like a pyramid.

were planned and used. The initial plan was fairly simple. It called for the door in the structure's north side to lead into a tunnel that slanted downward. Archaeologists dubbed it the Descending Corridor. This 221-foot (67m) passage led to a burial chamber that was 98 feet (30m) below the pyramid.

But at some point during the construction, Khufu and his architect changed their minds. For reasons only they knew, they chose to make a new burial chamber. It was higher up, inside the pyramid itself. To reach it, workers made a tunnel that slanted upward. Today it is called the Ascending Corridor. It led to a second burial chamber that was 19 feet (5.8m) long, 17 feet (5.2m) wide, and 20 feet (6.1m) high.

As it turned out, that second chamber, the queen's chamber, was also abandoned. Still higher up inside the pyramid, the builders made a third burial chamber. This one, known as the King's Chamber,

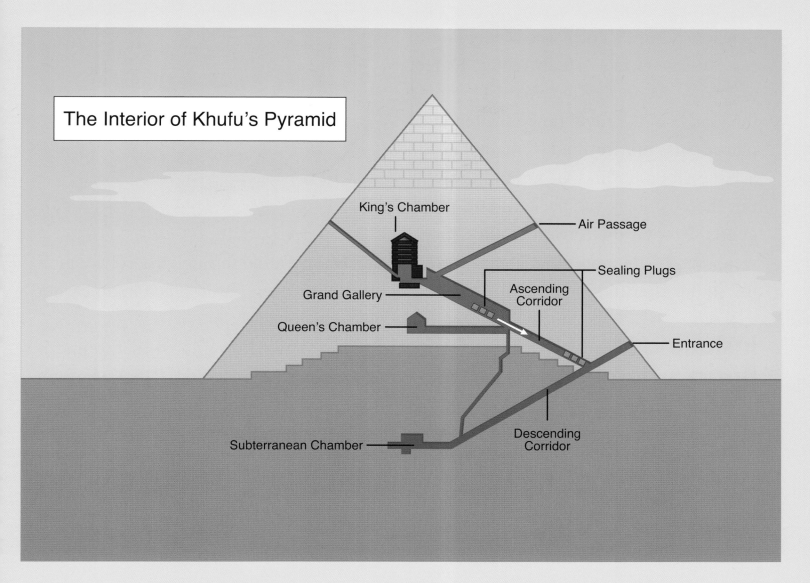

The Interior of Khufu's Pyramid

King's Chamber

Air Passage

Sealing Plugs

Grand Gallery

Ascending Corridor

Queen's Chamber

Entrance

Descending Corridor

Subterranean Chamber

is where Khufu's body was finally laid to rest. It was 34 feet (10.4m) long, 17 feet (5.2m) wide, and 19 feet (5.8m) high. At the climax of the royal funeral, attendants placed his **mummified** remains inside a large stone coffin. All around the coffin, the chamber was packed with grave goods. Among them were clothes, food, weapons, boats, and other items for his use in the afterlife.

Installing the Burial Chamber

When archaeologists first examined the King's Chamber, they saw something odd about Khufu's stone coffin. It was wider than the room's doorway to the Ascending Corridor. That meant that the workers could not have carried it into the

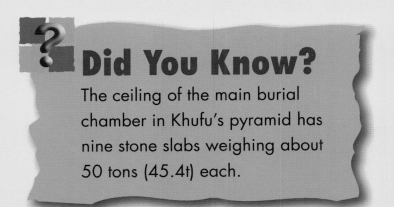

Did You Know?

The ceiling of the main burial chamber in Khufu's pyramid has nine stone slabs weighing about 50 tons (45.4t) each.

finished pyramid through the corridors. It must have been put in place in an earlier phase of construction.

This showed how most of the interior spaces were installed. They were not dug out after the structure was finished. Instead, the builders made them as the pyramid rose. The architect waited until the rising courses of stone reached a certain point. Then he marked a rectangular outline in the center of the topmost

Making Mummies

Like many other ancient Egyptians, Khufu and other pharaohs were mummified before burial. The belief was that part of the soul stayed in the body after death. So it was vital to preserve the remains as long as possible. The **embalmers** began by taking out most of a body's internal organs. They put them in a special jar. Then they lowered the body into a tub of mineral salt. Over several weeks the salt removed most of the body's moisture. Next, the embalmers washed the corpse and wrapped it in long strips of cloth. Finally, the person's relatives and friends put the mummy in a coffin inside a tomb. They placed the jar holding the organs near the coffin.

During the mummification process Egyptian embalmers placed the internal organs of the deceased in a jar next to the coffin.

course. This, he told the workers, would be the floor of the King's Chamber. Next, he had them build the walls and ceiling of the chamber.

At that instant, the King's Chamber looked like a small, freestanding building. It rested in the middle of the topmost course of the unfinished pyramid. Finally, the workers added new courses of stone around and on top of the chamber. In this way, they concealed it within the growing structure.

Lines of Defense

There is a reason that the burial chamber is surrounded by thousands of tons of solid rock. This was to make sure tomb robbers could not get in. Another security feature was the way the build-ers sealed off the entrance to the chamber after the royal funeral. They placed three huge and heavy slabs of granite in front of it. Then they blocked the corridor leading to the chamber with more huge chunks of stone.

There was still another line of defense against thieves. The architect and a handful of workers put a casing stone over the outer door on the pyramid's north face. Once it was in place, only those few people knew which casing stone covered the entrance. They hoped its exact location would be forgotten over time. If they had been able to see into the future, they would have been shocked. All their efforts to protect the royal corpse would one day come to nothing.

Chapter 4

The Pyramids in Later Ages

The story of the Giza pyramids after the Pyramid Age starts on a troubled note. In spite of all the precautions the builders had taken, tomb robbers were able to get inside. The bodies and treasures of Khufu and his fellow pharaohs were stolen. As time went on, the emptied pyramids also suffered from neglect and lack of repair.

But this sad story has a happy ending. Over the centuries, the pyramids' fortunes reversed. They regained much of their glory. Today they are hailed as wonders of the modern world as well as the ancient one.

Robbers Loot the Pyramids

The pyramids' builders put a lot of time and effort into making them safe from thieves. So why did these efforts fail? Part of the answer lies with how well they were guarded. In the years

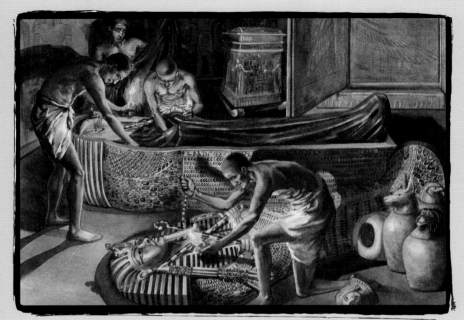

When Egyptian society became unstable, the pyramids became victims of large-scale looting. Thieves not only robbed tombs but also the limestone facings of the structures.

But several years after Menkaure's reign in the late 2000s BC, Egypt entered a time of troubles. The country became disunited. There were violent power struggles for the throne. Law and order broke down. Also, the men vying for power did not see guarding old tombs as worth the money and effort. So tomb robbers had no one to stop them and they tunneled into the Giza pyramids and looted them.

More time passed, and Egypt regained peace and stability. But now it was the government's turn to deface the old monuments. Builders needed limestone

immediately after they were built, armed guards likely watched over them day and night. This kept any would-be thieves away. Security stayed tight as long as Egypt was stable. With strong rulers and a good economy, law and order prevailed. And the Giza pyramids stayed safe.

for new tombs and other structures. But the national treasury was short of money. So the government started stripping the limestone casing stones from the Giza pyramids.

Century upon Century

Still more years, including the reigns of dozens of pharaohs, passed. The three great pyramids continued to tower over the Giza plateau. But by now, no one took care of them anymore. So decade by decade, century upon century, weathering and decay slowly took a toll on them.

Even so, they retained their huge size. Indeed, the giants of Giza remained awesome sights. As a result, they were still popular with tourists. Travelers from other lands visited them from time to time. Among them was Herodotus, who arrived sometime in the 450s BC.

But it was hard to get accurate facts about the towering stone structures. The builders' names were still known. But after so many centuries, no one could recall many details about them. No one knew when the pyramids were built. This is why Herodotus wrote down so much wrong information about them.

Not much changed in the years that followed. In 130 BC, nearly three centuries after Herodotus's death, another Greek visited Giza. His name was Antipater of Sidon. He was making a list of what he viewed as the seven great wonders of the known world. Struck almost

The Greek historian Herodotus toured Egypt in the 450s BC and wrote about the wonder of the pyramids.

speechless by the sight of Khufu's pyramid, he wasted no time in adding it to his list.

A Primitive People?

Some six centuries or so after Antipater's day, the ancient era ended. It was followed by the 1,000-year-long medieval period. During this time, foreigners ruled Egypt. They had little or no interest in Egypt's past glories. Neither did their mostly poor and **illiterate** subjects. So they did not maintain the country's many ancient monuments. Thus, these once dazzling structures continued to decay and fall apart. The Giza pyramids were much bigger and better built than most others. This is partly why these huge tombs remained largely intact while the ancient palaces and temples crumbled around them.

Poverty and neglect continued to thrive in Egypt. By early modern times, it was a very poor and backward country. In the 1700s and 1800s, no one remembered who had built the Giza pyramids. In fact, by this time even their original purpose had been forgotten.

Europeans and others continued to visit the pyramids. Most were very impressed. But many of these visitors were shocked by the poverty and lack of education in Egypt. They thought the Egyptians were, and always had been, a primitive people.

Did You Know?

Because of a high rate of accidents in the past, today one must get special permission to climb the Giza pyramids.

So they found it hard to believe their ancestors had built structures as splendid as the Giza pyramids. Some Europeans even claimed that the Egyptians had not built the pyramids. One writer said that the biblical character Noah had done it.

History's Great Wheel

By the early 1900s such theories had been proved wrong. Archaeologists showed that the Egyptians had long ago created a powerful and brilliant

A Prison for Angels

In 1846 English novelist Harriet Martineau visited Khufu's great pyramid. At the time, few Western women had the courage to climb to the top of the structure or enter its dark inner chambers. She did both. She later recalled the strong impression the enormous King's Chamber made on her, writing in her book *Eastern Life, Present and Past*, "There is nothing like it. No catacomb or cavern in the world. There never was, and surely there never will be…. The fantastic character of its walls and roofs takes off from the impression of its vastness and gloom. Here, the [gloom is so deep] as to make this seem like a fit prison-house for angels."

English writer and social reformer Harriet Martineau visited Khufu's pyramid in 1846.

civilization. Plenty of evidence showed that some of the pharaohs were great builders. And among their greatest projects were the giant structures at Giza. The evidence also showed that these monuments were those rulers' tombs.

After many centuries, the ancient Egyptians had finally gotten the credit they deserved. This happened at a time when the country was quickly becoming more modern. More and more Egyptians rose from poverty and became educated. These new generations took deep pride in the Giza pyramids. Those structures became both proof of Egypt's glorious past and the chief symbols of the modern Egyptian nation.

In the meantime, the Giza pyramids continued to draw tourists from

The "Chosen" Race

Many early modern Europeans doubted that the Egyptians had built the pyramids. One was British scientist Charles Piazzi Smyth. He wrote a book in 1864 called *Our Inheritance in the Great Pyramid* about the Giza pyramids. In it he said the non–Judeo Christian Egyptians were incapable of building such magnificent structures. Instead, he claimed, they were built by the Hebrews. Moreover, God had directly helped his "chosen" people in the project. The builders "were by no means Egyptians," Smyth insisted. Rather, they were members of "the chosen race, descendants of [the prophet] Abraham." Experts now know that Smythe was wrong. Abundant evidence confirms that the Egyptians did erect the pyramids.

around the globe. Most were amazed at their huge size. Added to that was their simplicity and elegance. The fact that

Modern Copies of the Pyramids

A glass pyramid marks the entrance to Paris's Louvre museum. It is one of many modern structures inspired by the pyramids at Giza. The Luxor Hotel in Las Vegas, Nevada, is another. The hotel has a 30-story version of Khufu's pyramid. Still another modern version of that ancient tomb is the Palace of Peace and Reconciliation. It stands 203 feet (77m) tall in downtown Astana, the capital of Kazakhstan.

The pyramids of Egypt have inspired many architects of modern structures, among them the Luxor Hotel in Las Vegas, Nevada.

A reconstruction of the Giza Pyramid complex in ancient times.

people without modern machines had built them also seemed remarkable. All of these factors gave the pyramids a kind of nobility. And this inspired emotional reactions in many who gazed on them.

Modern artists and architects were also inspired by the pyramids. In the late 20th century, designers copied their form in buildings around the world. One good example can be seen at the famous Louvre museum in Paris, France. A shining glass pyramid rises at its entrance.

Such tributes emphasize the pyramids' survival and ultimate triumph. The great civilization that built them vanished long ago. Yet through countless centuries of neglect, they endured. And today they stand guard over a newly dynamic Egyptian people. For the pyramids, the great wheel of history has truly come full circle.

Glossary

aligning [uh-LINE-ing]: Setting up or placing something in a certain way.

archaeologists [ARK-eh-AHL-uh-jistz]: People who dig up and study lost civilizations.

ben-ben [BEN-ben]: In Egyptian mythology, the original mound of creation.

cardinal points [CARD-in-l pointz]: The directions north, south, east, and west.

courses [COR-sez]: In a building, layers of stones or other building materials.

embalmers [em-BAHM-erz]: People who mummify, or embalm, bodies.

funerary [FEW-ner-air-ee]: Having to do with funerals and death.

grave goods [grave goodz]: Food, clothes, tools, and other items that ancient peoples placed inside tombs so the deceased could use them in the afterlife.

horizontal [hor-i-ZON-tl]: Running from side to side.

illiterate [ill-LIT-er-it]: Unable to read and write.

levers [LEV-erz]: Sticks or poles used to lift heavy objects by putting one end under an object and pushing the stick or pole up or down.

mastabas [muh-STAH-buz]: In ancient Egypt, flat-topped rectangular tombs made of mud bricks or stone.

mummified [MUM-uh-fide]: Describes a body that has gone through a process for preserving it after death.

pharaohs [FAY-rowz]: The kings of ancient Egypt.

resurrection [rez-er-REK-shun]: The process of a person coming back to life after death.

sledges [SLEJ-iz]: Sled-shaped containers with which ancient peoples moved heavy objects.

symbols [SIM-bulls]: Things that stand for or represent something else.

vizier [vuh-ZEER]: In ancient Egypt, the pharaoh's chief administrator.

zaa [ZAH]: In ancient Egypt, construction gangs containing 200 men.

For More Information

Books

Crispin Boyer
Everything Ancient Egypt.
Washington, DC: National
Geographic, 2012.

Anita Croy, ed.
Ancient Egypt. Redding, CT: Brown
Bear, 2010.

Christopher Forest
Pyramids of Ancient Egypt. Mankato,
MN: Capstone, 2012.

Jen Green
Ancient Egypt. New York: Dorling
Kindersley, 2008.

Brianna Hall
Mummies of Ancient Egypt. Mankato,
MN: Capstone, 2012.

Kate Riggs
Egyptian Pyramids. Mankato, MN:
Creative Education, 2009.

Websites

Ancient Egypt

www.ancient-egypt.org

Building in Ancient Egypt

www.reshafim.org.il/ad/egypt/building

Discovery of the Tombs of the Pyramid Builders at Giza

www.guardians.net/hawass/buildtomb.htm

Great Pyramid of Khufu

www.greatbuildings.com/buildings/Great_Pyramid.html

Mummy Maker

www.bbc.co.uk/history/ancient/egyptians/mummy_maker_game.shtml

Pyramids: The Inside Story

www.pbs.org/wgbh/nova/pyramid

Index

A

Afterlife, 6, 7, 21, 32
Antipater of Sidon, 37

B

Ben-ben (sacred mound), 27, 30

D

Djoser (pharaoh), *8*, 9, 11, 12
  pyramid of, 9, *10*, 11–12

E

Eastern Life, Present and Past (Martineau), 40
Egypt
  after ancient era, 39–40
  after Menkaure's reign, 36
Embalming, 33

F

Funerary writings, 27, 29

G

Giza pyramids, 4–5, *5*, 7
  after Pyramid Age, 35–38
  in modern times, 39–41, 43
  pyramid complex, *18, 43*
  quarrying stone for, 19
Grave goods, 7, 32
Great Sphinx (Giza), 25

H

Hawass, Zahi, 17
Herodotus, 15–16, 23, 26, 37, 38, *38*
Hieroglyphics, *28*

I

Imhotep (vizier), 9, 11, 26

K

Khafre (pharaoh), 12–13, 25
Khufu (pharaoh), 5–6, 7, 15
Khufu pyramid, 4, 5, *5*, 9, 12–13, 32
  interior of, 29–30, *31*, 32, 34

L

Levers, 19
Louvre, 43
Luxor Hotel (Las Vegas), 35, 42, *42*

M

Martineau, Harriet, 40, *40*
Mastabas (tombs), 7, 9
  at Saqqâra, 11–12
Menkaure (pharaoh), 13, 36
Mummies, 32, 33, *33*

O
Osiris (deity), 6, *6*

P
Pyramid Age (2667 BC–2180
  BC), 12–13
Pyramid Texts, 27, *29*
Pyramids
  construction of, 14–24 *20*
  dating of, 11
  looting of, 35–36
  modern copies of, 42
  origin of word, 27

spiritual elements of, 26–27
See also specific pyramids

R
Religion, 25–26

S
Sacred mounds, 27, 30
Sledges, 19
Smyth, Charles Piazzi, 41
Sneferu, 12
Step Pyramid (Saqqâra), *9,
  10*, 11–12

Stones
  quarrying of, 19
  raising of, 21, *22*, 23–24

W
Workers, 14–16
  incentives for, 21
  tools, 19
Workers' villages, 16–17

Z
Zaa (gangs), 18, *24*

About the Author

Historian and award-winning writer Don Nardo has published numerous books for young people about the ancient world. They cover the histories, cultures, religions, myths, and daily lives of the Babylonians, Egyptians, Greeks, Romans, and other peoples of the distant past. For lists of and information about his books, see his website at Nardopublishing.com.